Eating Vegetarian

50 Most Wanted Healthy and Tasty Recipes For Your Vegetarian Cooking

ANNIE HART

TABLE OF CONTENTS

INTRODUCTION

A large number of individuals who have deliberately inspected creature agribusiness have made plans to go veggie lover. In any case, regardless of whether you choose a veggie lover diet isn't for you, you'll likely leave away from perusing this exposition sold on the advantages of eating what individuals currently call a "plant-based" diet. For what reason am I so sure? Since the motivations to pick an eating routine that is at any rate generally plant-based are overpowering to such an extent that there truly aren't any solid counterarguments. That may clarify why the most unmistakable nourishment governmental issues journalists—including Michael Pollan, Mark Bittman, and Eric Schlosser—advocate an eating routine dependent on plants.

Plant-based weight control plans convey a significant number of the advantages of being vegetarian while requiring just the scarcest exertion. Since you haven't dedicated yourself to being 100 percent anything, there's no motivation to stress that you'll cheat, slip, or mess up. You can follow a plant-based eating routine and still eat Thanksgiving turkey or a late spring grill. In the event that being 100 percent veggie lover is something individuals focus on, being plant-based is more something they incline toward.

Perhaps the best thing about the plant-based idea is that it frequently gets under way an "idealistic cycle," where one positive change prompts another and afterward to another. At the point when you normally attempt new veggie lover nourishments, your top picks will in general consequently become piece of your ordinary eating regimen. So as time passes by, your eating regimen will probably move in a veggie lover heading with no deliberate exertion on your part. A lot of current veggie lovers arrived by bit by bit sliding down the plant-based slant. After some time spent eating expanding measures of plant-based nourishments, they understood that they were only a couple of little and simple advances from turning out to be absolutely vegetarian.

There are various adorable and accommodating neologisms appended to the plant-based camp: reducetarian, flexitarian, chegan, plant-solid, and even veganish. On the off chance that any of these terms impacts you, simply snatch tightly to it and start thinking thusly as you start attempting more veggie lover and vegetarian suppers.

Also, there are a few other related ideas you may discover supportive, including: Meatless Mondays, Mark Bittman's Vegan Before 6:00 arrangement, or taking a completely vegetarian diet out for a 21-day test drive. These conceivable outcomes can move huge change without forcing prerequisites for long lasting flawlessness.

Of the numerous motivations to go plant-based, maybe the best of all is the absence of a reasonable counterargument. In the entirety of my years expounding on nourishment legislative issues, I've not even once observed anybody (other than a couple paleo diet fan) make a genuine endeavor to contend against eating for the most part plants, since the preferences are unquestionable. Handfuls and many examinations show that eating more products of the soil can drastically diminish paces of malignant growth, diabetes, and circulatory malady. Furthermore, obviously, plant-based weight control plans likewise keep livestock from butcher, while all the while securing nature.

BREAKFAST & SMOOTHIES

01. Sweet Coffee and Cacao Smoothie

Preparation time: 3 minutes

Servings 2

Ingredients

- 2 tsp Coffee
- ½ a Banana
- 1 cup Almond Milk
- 1 tsp Cashew Butter
- 2 tsp Cacao Powder
- 1 tsp maple Syrup
- 1 scoop vegan protein powder
- ½ cup Chocolate

Directions:

1. Pop everything in a blender and blitz
2. Pour into glasses and serve.

Nutrition:

Calories 614, Total Fat 43.2g, Saturated Fat 34.6g, Cholesterol 10mg, Sodium 146mg, Total Carbohydrate 44.7g, Dietary Fiber 5.4g, Total Sugars 31.2g, Protein 17.6g, Vitamin D 0mcg, Calcium 104mg, Iron 4mg, Potassium 614mg

02. Amazing Blueberry Smoothie

Preparation time: 5 minutes
Servings 2

Ingredients:

- ½ avocado
- 1 cup frozen blueberries
- 1 cup raw spinach
- ¼ tsp sea salt
- 1 cup soy
- 1 frozen banana

Directions:

1. Blend everything in a powerful blender until you have a smooth, creamy shake.
2. Enjoy your healthy shake and start your morning on a fresh note!

Nutrition:

Calories 269, Total Fat 12.3g, Saturated Fat 2.3g, Cholesterol 0mg, Sodium 312mg, Total Carbohydrate 37.6g, Dietary Fiber 8.2g, Total Sugars 22.9g, Protein 6.4g, Vitamin D 0mcg, Calcium 52mg, Iron 3mg, Potassium 528mg

03. Go-Green Smoothie

Preparation time: 5 minutes
Servings 1

Ingredients:

- 2 tablespoons, natural cashew butter
- 1 ripe banana
- 2/3 cup, unsweetened coconut
- ½ cup kale

Directions:

1. Put everything inside a powerful blender.
2. Blend until you have a smooth, creamy shake.
3. Enjoy your special green smoothie.

Nutrition:

Calories 500, Total Fat 33.2g, Saturated Fat 18.9g, Cholesterol 0mg, Sodium 161mg, Total Carbohydrate 48.6g, Dietary Fiber 10.4g, Total Sugars 19.8g, Protein 9.1g, Vitamin D 0mcg, Calcium 72mg, Iron 9mg, Potassium 777mg

04. Creamy Chocolate Shake

Preparation time: 10 minutes

Servings 2

Ingredients:

- 2 frozen ripe bananas, chopped
- 1/3 cup frozen strawberries
- 2 tbsp cocoa powder
- 2 tbsp salted almond butter
- 2 cups unsweetened vanilla almond milk
- 1 dash Stevia or agave nectar
- 1/3 cup ice

Directions:

1. Add all ingredients in a blender and blend until smooth.
2. Take out and serve.

Nutrition:

Calories 272, Total Fat 14.3g, Saturated Fat 1.5g, Cholesterol 0mg, Sodium 315mg, Total Carbohydrate 37g, Dietary Fiber 7.3g, Total Sugars 16.8g, Protein 6.2g, Vitamin D 2mcg, Calcium 735mg, Iron 2mg, Potassium 732mg

05. Hidden Kale Smoothie

Preparation time: 5 minutes

Servings 2

Ingredients:

- 1 medium ripe banana, peeled and sliced
- ½ cup frozen mixed berries
- 1 tbsp hulled hemp seeds
- 2 cups frozen or fresh kale
- 2/3 cup 100% pomegranate juice
- 2¼ cups filtered water

Directions:

1. Add all ingredients in a blender and blend until smooth.
2. Take out and serve.

Nutrition:

Calories 164, Total Fat 2g, Saturated Fat 0.2g, Cholesterol 0mg, Sodium 51mg, Total Carbohydrate 34.2g, Dietary Fiber 3.9g, Total Sugars 17.7g, Protein 4.1g, Vitamin D 0mcg, Calcium 124mg, Iron 2mg, Potassium 776mg

MAINS

01. Risotto With Tomato & Herbs

Preparation Time: 10 minutes

Cooking Time: 20 minutes

Servings: 32

Ingredients:

- 2 oz. Arborio rice
- 1 teaspoon dried garlic, minced
- 3 tablespoons dried onion, minced
- 1 tablespoon dried Italian seasoning, crushed
- ¾ cup snipped dried tomatoes
- 1 ½ cups reduced-sodium chicken broth

Directions:

1. Make the dry risotto mix by combining all the ingredients except broth in a large bowl.
2. Divide the mixture into eight resealable plastic bags. Seal the bag.
3. Store at room temperature for up to 3 months.
4. When ready to serve, pour the broth in a pot.
5. Add the contents of 1 plastic bag of dry risotto mix.
6. Bring to a boil and then reduce heat.
7. Cover the pot and simmer for 20 minutes.
8. Serve with vegetables.

Nutritional Value:
Calories 80
Total Fat 0 g
Saturated Fat 0 g
Cholesterol 0 mg
Sodium 276 mg
Total Carbohydrate 17 g
Dietary Fiber 2 g
Total Sugars 0 g
Protein 3 g
Potassium 320 mg

02. Tofu Shawarma Rice

Preparation Time: 15 minutes
Cooking Time: 15 minutes
Servings: 4

Ingredients:

- 4 cups cooked brown rice
- 4 cups cooked tofu, sliced into small cubes
- 4 cups cucumber, cubed
- 4 cups tomatoes, cubed
- 4 cups white onion, cubed
- 2 cups cabbage, shredded
- 1/2 cup vegan mayo
- 1/8 cup garlic, minced
- Garlic salt to taste
- Hot sauce

Directions:

1. Add brown rice into 4 food containers.
2. Arrange tofu, cucumber, tomatoes, white onion and cabbage on top.
3. In a bowl, mix the mayo, garlic, and garlic salt.
4. Drizzle top with garlic sauce and hot sauce before serving.

Nutritional Value:
Calories 667
Total Fat 12.6g
Saturated Fat 2.2g
Cholesterol 0mg
Sodium 95mg
Total Carbohydrate 116.5g
Dietary Fiber 9.9g
Total Sugars 9.4g
Protein 26.1g
Potassium 1138mg

03. Pesto Pasta

Preparation Time: 10 minutes
Cooking Time: 8 minutes
Servings: 2

Ingredients:
- 1 cup fresh basil leaves
- 4 cloves garlic
- 2 tablespoons walnut
- 2 tablespoons olive oil
- 1 tablespoon vegan Parmesan cheese
- 2 cups cooked penne pasta
- 2 tablespoons black olives, sliced

Directions:
1. Put the basil leaves, garlic, walnut, olive oil and Parmesan cheese in a food processor.
2. Pulse until smooth.
3. Divide pasta into 2 food containers.
4. Spread the basil sauce on top.
5. Top with black olives.
6. Store until ready to serve.

Nutritional Value:
Calories 374
Total Fat 21.1g
Saturated Fat 2.6g
Cholesterol 47mg
Sodium 92mg
Total Carbohydrate 38.6g
Dietary Fiber 1.1g
Total Sugars 0.2g
Protein 10g
Potassium 215mg

04. "Cheesy" Spinach Rolls

Preparation Time: 20 minutes
Cooking Time: 15 minutes
Servings: 6

Ingredients:

- 18 spinach leaves
- 18 vegan spring roll wrappers
- 6 slices cheese, cut into 18 smaller strips
- Water
- 1 cup vegetable oil
- 6 cups cauliflower rice
- 3 cups tomato, cubed
- 3 cups cucumber, cubed
- 1 tablespoon olive oil
- 1 teaspoon balsamic vinegar

Directions:

1. Place one spinach leaf on top of each wrapper.
2. Add a small strip of vegan cheese on top of each spinach leaf.
3. Roll the wrapper and seal the edges with water.
4. In a pan over medium high heat, add the vegetable oil.
5. Cooking Time: the rolls until golden brown.
6. Drain in paper towels.

7. Divide cauliflower rice into 6 food containers.
8. Add 3 cheesy spinach rolls in each food container.
9. Toss cucumber and tomato in olive oil and vinegar.
10. Place the cucumber tomato relish beside the rolls.
11. Seal and reheat in the microwave when ready to serve.

Nutritional Value:
Calories 746
Total Fat 38.5g
Saturated Fat 10.1g
Cholesterol 33mg
Sodium 557mg
Total Carbohydrate 86.2g
Dietary Fiber 3.8g
Total Sugars 2.6g
Protein 18g
Potassium 364mg

05. Grilled Summer Veggies

Preparation Time: 15 minutes
Cooking Time: 6 minutes
Servings: 6

Ingredients:

- 2 teaspoons cider vinegar
- 1 tablespoon olive oil
- ¼ teaspoon fresh thyme, chopped
- 1 teaspoon fresh parsley, chopped
- ¼ teaspoon fresh rosemary, chopped
- Salt and pepper to taste
- 1 onion, sliced into wedges
- 2 red bell peppers, sliced
- 3 tomatoes, sliced in half
- 6 large mushrooms, stems removed
- 1 eggplant, sliced crosswise
- 3 tablespoons olive oil
- 1 tablespoon cider vinegar

Directions:

1. Make the dressing by mixing the vinegar, oil, thyme, parsley, rosemary, salt and pepper.
2. In a bowl, mix the onion, red bell pepper, tomatoes, mushrooms and eggplant.
3. Toss in remaining olive oil and cider vinegar.
4. Grill over medium heat for 3 minutes.
5. Turn the vegetables and grill for another 3 minutes.
6. Arrange grilled vegetables in a food container.
7. Drizzle with the herbed mixture when ready to serve.

Nutritional Value:

Calories 127
Total Fat 9 g
Saturated Fat 1 g
Cholesterol 0 mg
Sodium 55 mg
Total Carbohydrate 11 g
Dietary Fiber 5 g
Total Sugars 5 g
Protein 3 g
Potassium 464 mg

SIDES AND SALADS

01. Roasted Broccoli With Peanuts And Kecap Manis

Preparation Time: 40 minutes
Servings: 4

Ingredients

- Broccoli: a large head diced
- Vegetable oil: 1 tbsp
- Kecap manis: 4 tbsp
- Spring onions: 2 sliced
- Grated garlic: 2 cloves
- Sesame oil: 2 tbsp
- Ginger: 1 tbsp grated
- Dried chili flakes: a pinch
- Salted peanuts: a handful roughly chopped
- Rice vinegar: 3 tbsp
- Coriander: ½ cup chopped
- Ready-made crispy onions: 3 tbsp
- Water: 50ml
- Cooked jasmine rice to serve

Directions:
1. Preheat the oven to 180C
2. Take a large pan and add oil and fry broccoli in batches and spread on baking sheet
3. In the same pan, fry garlic, ginger, and chili flakes for a minute and then add rice vinegar, manis, sesame oil, and water
4. Pour all of this mixture over broccoli and cover with foil
5. Roast the broccoli for 20 minutes in the oven
6. Mix crispy onion and salted peanuts together and sprinkle over cooked broccoli
7. Top with coriander and serve with rice

Nutrition:
Carbs: 22.5 g
Protein: 9.4 g
Fats: 12.8 g
Calories:258 Kcal

02. Roasted Red Cabbage Pesto

Preparation Time: 10 minutes

Servings: 4 as a side dish

Ingredients

- Red cabbage: 1 head small
- Garlic: 2 cloves
- Lemon juice: 3 tbsp
- Ground almonds: 2 tbsp
- Extra-virgin olive oil: 3 tbsp
- Salt: as per your need
- Chili sauce: 1 tbsp

Directions:

1. Roast cabbage in the oven for 10 minutes at 160C
2. Take a blender and add all the ingredients including roasted cabbage
3. Blend them well
4. Serve with crispy chips

Nutrition:

Carbs: 11.8g

Protein: 10.4g

Fats: 34.2g

Calories: 366Kcal

03. Roasted Garlic Toasts

Preparation Time: 45 minutes

Servings: 4

Ingredients

- Whole bulbs garlic: 4
- Olive oil: 400ml
- Cherry tomatoes: 300g halved
- Sprigs thyme: 6
- Toasted sourdough: 4 slices

Directions:

1. Preheat the oven to medium heat
2. Cut the garlic horizontally and sprinkle thyme and salt, and add to the bowl filled with oil
3. Place in the oven and Cooking Time: for 25 minutes till garlic becomes soft
4. Remove from the oven and spread on the toasted sourdough
5. Top with cherry tomatoes and serve

Nutrition:

Carbs: 38 g

Protein: 8.8 g

Fats: 18.2 g

Calories: 358 Kcal

04. Roasted Olive Oil Tomatoes

Preparation Time: 1 hour 50 minutes
Servings: 5

Ingredients

- Cherry tomatoes on the vine: 4-6 bunches
- Bay leaves: 6
- Olive oil: 200ml
- Garlic: 1 whole bulb cut in ½
- Crusty bread warmed to serve

Directions:

1. Heat the oven to 150C
2. Put the garlic and tomatoes in a baking dish, now add bay leaves and season
3. Pour the olive oil on a baking dish and cover it with foil
4. Let it bake for 1 ½ hour and then serve it with crusty bread

Nutrition:

Carbs: 4.6g
Protein: 1.3g
Fats: 33.6g
Calories: 328Kcal

05. Rocket Chickpeas Salad

Preparation Time: 15 minutes

Servings: 2

Ingredients

- Avocado: 1 cut into small pieces
- Chickpeas: 400g can drained and rinsed
- Red chili: 1 chopped
- Cumin seeds: 1 tsp
- Red onion: 1/2 finely chopped
- Roasted red peppers: 3 chopped
- Olive oil
- Lime: 1 plus wedges to serve
- Rocket: 2 handfuls
- Pitta bread: 2 warmed

Directions:

1. Mix onion, avocado, peppers, chickpeas, and chili in a bowl
2. Take two tablespoons of olive oil and whisk it with lime juice while adding seasoning and cumin seeds
3. Put it in the bowl and mix well
4. Add the chickpeas mixture to the rocket pile into 2 plates
5. Best served with warm pittas

Nutrition: Carbs: 60.4g ,Protein: 18.3g ,Fats: 26.4g , Calories: 586Kcal

SOUPS AND STEWS

01. Brown Lentils Tomato Soup

Preparation Time: 40 minutes

Servings: 2

Ingredients

- Brown lentils: 1 cup
- Crushed tomatoes: 2 cups
- Onion: 1 diced
- Ginger: 1 tbsp paste
- Garlic: 1 tbsp paste
- Vegetable oil: 2 tbsp
- Water: 4 cups
- Italian herb seasoning: 1 tbsp
- Salt & pepper: as per your taste

Directions:

1. Take a large saucepan and add oil on a medium flame
2. Add onion and ginger and garlic paste and sauté for 3-4 minutes
3. Pour water and bring to boil
4. Add lentils and salt and bring to boil
5. Lower the heat to medium and Cooking Time: for 20 minutes with partial cover

6. Now add crushed tomatoes to the lentils along with herb seasoning and pepper
7. Cooking Time: on low flame for 15 minutes
8. Add the mixture to the high speed blender to make puree
9. Add salt and pepper to augment taste

Nutrition:
Carbs: 30.8g
Protein: 12.7g
Fats: 15.2g
Calories: 323.2Kcal

02. Brown Lentils Green Veggies Combo Soup

Preparation Time: 1 hour

Servings: 4-6

Ingredients

- Brown lentils: 150g
- Chickpeas: 400g can drained and rinsed
- Onion: 1 large finely chopped
- Leek: 2 diced
- Parsnips: 2 large finely diced
- Kale: 85g leaves shredded
- Olive oil: 2 tbsp
- Garlic: 2 cloves crushed
- Cayenne pepper: 1 tsp
- Coriander: a small bunch finely sliced
- Ground cinnamon: 1 tsp
- Ground turmeric: 1 tsp
- Ground coriander: 2 tsp
- Vegetable stock: 1 liter
- Lemons juice: 2 tbsp
- Salt: as per your need

Directions:

1. Take a large pan and heat olive oil in it
2. Add onions and parsnips and Cooking Time: them for 10 minutes
3. Then add coriander stalks and garlic and

Cooking Time: for a minute and mix well

4. Next add spices and stir in lentils
5. Pour the stock and boil and then cover and Cooking Time: for 20 minutes and add leek at 10 minutes
6. Remove the lid and add in kale and chickpeas and stir
7. Sprinkle salt and pour in lemon juice
8. Top with coriander and serve

Nutrition: Carbs: 29.4 g , Protein: 12.8 g , Fats: 7.2 g ,Calories: 258 Kcal

03. Cannellini Beans Tomato Soup

Preparation Time: 30 minutes
Servings: 2

Ingredients

- Cannellini beans: 1 cup can
- Tomatoes: 1 cup chunks
- Tomatoes: 1 cup can
- Tomato paste: 2 tbsp
- Oregano: 2 tbsp dried
- Onion: 1 (finely chopped
- Garlic: 3 cloves (crushed
- Fresh basil: 1 small bunch
- Vegetable broth: 4 cups
- Salt & pepper: as per your taste
- Olive oil: 2 tbsp

Directions:

1. Take a large saucepan, heat olive oil in it
2. Add onion and garlic in it
3. Include tomato chunks, can chopped tomatoes, and tomato paste and combine them all together
4. Now add vegetable broth, oregano and fresh basil
5. Bring the mixture to boil and then lower the

heat to medium and Cooking Time: for 15 minutes

6. Use the hand blender to blend the soup content and season with salt and pepper
7. Rinse, dry, and roast the cannellini beans
8. Add these beans on top of the soup and serve hot

Nutrition:
Carbs: 40g
Protein: 13.87g
Fats: 18.05g
Calories: 385.7Kcal

04. Cashew Chickpeas Soup

Preparation Time: 25 minutes

Servings: 2

Ingredients

- Chickpeas: 1 cup can
- Cashew nuts: ½ cup
- Spinach: 2 cups chopped
- Onion: 1 medium
- Freshly grated ginger: 2 tbsp
- Curry powder: 1 tbsp mild
- Vegetable broth: 2 cups
- Olive oil: 2 tbsp
- Lemon juice: as per your taste
- Garlic: 3 cloves
- Salt: as per your taste
- Fresh coriander: 2 tbsp

Directions:

1. Take a large pan and add olive oil
2. Add onion and garlic and fry for a minute and add curry powder and ginger
3. Continue frying for 5 minutes to make onion soft
4. Add spinach and vegetable broth and Cooking Time: on a medium flame for 10 minutes

5. Now blend with the hand blender and add sliced cashews and chickpeas
6. Add water if needed and simmer for 5 minutes
7. Serve with lemon juice and fresh coriander on top

Nutrition:
Carbs: 24.03g
Protein: 12.16g
Fats: 21.26g
Calories: 309 Kcal

05. Charred Mexican Sweetcorn Soup

Preparation Time: 45 minutes

Servings: 4

Ingredients

- Corn on the cob: 2
- Dried ancho chili: 1
- Onion: 1 finely chopped
- Vegetable stock: 1 liter
- Celery: 2 sticks finely chopped
- Ground cumin: 2 tsp
- Roasted red peppers: 4 chopped
- Garlic: 3 cloves finely chopped
- Sweet smoked paprika: 2 tsp
- Limes: 2 - 1 juice and other wedged to serve
- Vegetable oil: 2 tbsp
- Coriander: a small bunch chopped

Directions:

1. Take a bowl and add ancho chili and pour boiling water from the top
2. Leave the mixture for 10 minutes and then remove stem and seed
3. Take a pan and heat oil in it and add celery and onion and Cooking Time: for 10 minutes with

a pinch of salt

4. Add all the spices and Cooking Time: for a minute
5. Include now ancho chili, vegetable stock, and pepper and Cooking Time: for 15 minutes
6. Season with salt and blend the mixture
7. In the meanwhile, on a light heat Cooking Time: corns in the pan lightly brushed with salt, pepper, and oil
8. Cooking Time: the cobs for 10 minutes and then remove from heat
9. Use a sharp knife to remove corns and add to the soup
10. Sprinkle coriander on top and serve with lime juice

Nutrition: Carbs: 12.9 g
Protein: 5.6 g
Fats: 8.5 g
Calories: 162 Kcal

SOUPS, STEWS & CHILIES

01. Potato And Kale Soup

Preparation Time: 5 Minutes
Cooking Time: 50 Minutes
Servings: 4

Ingredients

- 1 tablespoon olive oil
- 1 medium onion, chopped
- 2 garlic cloves, minced
- 6 cups vegetable broth, homemade (see Light Vegetable Brothor store-bought, or water
- 2 large russet potatoes, peeled and cut into 1/2-inch dice
- 1/2 teaspoon dried oregano
- 1/4 teaspoon crushed red pepper
- 1 bay leaf
- Salt
- 4 cups chopped stemmed kale
- 11/2 cups cooked or 1 (15.5-ouncecan Great Northern beans, drained and rinsed

Directions

1. In a large pot, heat the oil over medium heat. Add the onion and garlic, cover, and Cooking Time: until softened, about 5 minutes. Add the broth, potatoes, oregano, crushed red pepper, bay leaf, and salt to taste, and bring to a boil. Reduce heat to low and simmer, uncovered, for 30 minutes.

2. Stir in the kale and the beans and Cooking Time: until the vegetables are tender, 15 to 20 minutes longer. Remove, discard the bay leaf, and serve.

02. Coconut Watercress Soup

Preparation Time: 10 Minutes
Cooking Time: 20 Minutes
Servings: 4

Ingredients
- 1 teaspoon coconut oil
- 1 onion, diced
- 2 cups fresh or frozen peas
- 4 cups water, or vegetable stock
- 1 cup fresh watercress, chopped
- 1 tablespoon fresh mint, chopped
- Pinch sea salt
- Pinch freshly ground black pepper
- ¾ cup coconut milk

Directions
1. Preparing the Ingredients.
2. Melt the coconut oil in a large pot over medium-high heat. Add the onion and Cooking Time: until soft, about 5 minutes, then add the peas and the water. Bring to a boil, then lower the heat and add the watercress, mint, salt, and pepper.
3. Cover and simmer for 5 minutes. Stir in the coconut milk, and purée the soup until smooth

in a blender or with an immersion blender.

4. Try this soup with any other fresh, leafy green—anything from spinach to collard greens to arugula to Swiss chard.

Nutrition: Calories: 178; Protein: 6g; Total fat: 10g; Carbohydrates: 18g; Fiber: 5g

03. Roasted Red Pepper And Butternut Squash Soup

Preparation Time: 10 Minutes
Cooking Time: 45 Minutes
Servings: 6

Ingredients

- 1 small butternut squash
- 1 tablespoon olive oil
- 1 teaspoon sea salt
- 2 red bell peppers
- 1 yellow onion
- 1 head garlic
- 2 cups water, or vegetable broth
- Zest and juice of 1 lime
- 1 to 2 tablespoons tahini
- Pinch cayenne pepper
- ½ teaspoon ground coriander
- ½ teaspoon ground cumin
- Toasted squash seeds (optional

Directions

1. Preparing the Ingredients.
2. Preheat the oven to 350°F.
3. Prepare the squash for roasting by cutting it in half lengthwise, scooping out the seeds, and poking some holes in the flesh with a fork.

Reserve the seeds if desired.

4. Rub a small amount of oil over the flesh and skin, then rub with a bit of sea salt and put the halves skin-side down in a large baking dish. Put it in the oven while you prepare the rest of the vegetables.

5. Prepare the peppers the exact same way, except they do not need to be poked.

6. Slice the onion in half and rub oil on the exposed faces. Slice the top off the head of garlic and rub oil on the exposed flesh.

7. After the squash has cooked for 20 minutes, add the peppers, onion, and garlic, and roast for another 20 minutes. Optionally, you can toast the squash seeds by putting them in the oven in a separate baking dish 10 to 15 minutes before the vegetables are finished.

8. Keep a close eye on them. When the vegetables are cooked, take them out and let them cool before handling them. The squash will be very soft when poked with a fork.

9. Scoop the flesh out of the squash skin into a large pot (if you have an immersion blenderor into a blender.

10. Chop the pepper roughly, remove the onion skin and chop the onion roughly, and squeeze the garlic cloves out of the head, all into the pot or blender. Add the water, the lime zest and juice, and the tahini. Purée the soup,

adding more water if you like, to your desired consistency. Season with the salt, cayenne, coriander, and cumin. Serve garnished with toasted squash seeds (if using).

Nutrition: Calories: 156; Protein: 4g; Total fat: 7g; Saturated fat: 11g; Carbohydrates: 22g; Fiber: 5g

04. Mushroom Medley Soup

Preparation Time: 5 Minutes
Cooking Time: 40 Minutes
Servings: 4 To 6

Ingredients

- 1 tablespoon olive oil
- 1 medium onion, chopped
- 1 large carrot, chopped
- 1 celery rib, chopped
- 8 ounces fresh shiitake mushrooms, lightly rinsed, patted dry, stemmed and cut into 1/4-inch slices
- 8 ounces cremini mushrooms, lightly rinsed, patted dry, and quartered
- 8 ounces white mushrooms, lightly rinsed, patted dry, and quartered
- 6 cups vegetable broth, mushroom broth, homemade
- 1/4 cup chopped fresh parsley
- 1 teaspoon minced fresh thyme or 1/2 teaspoon dried
- Salt and freshly ground black pepper

Directions

1. In a large pot, heat the oil over medium heat. Add the onion, carrot, and celery. Cover and Cooking Time: until softened, about 10 minutes. Stir in all the mushrooms and broth, and bring to boil.

2. Reduce heat to low, add the parsley and thyme, and season with salt and pepper to taste. Simmer, uncovered, until the vegetables are tender, about 30 minutes. Serve hot.

05. Tofu Coconut Indonesian Soup

Preparation Time: 10 Minutes

Servings: 4

Ingredients:

- 8ounces extra-firm tofu, cut into ½-inch dice
- 6ounces dried rice noodles
- 1(14-ouncecan coconut milk
- ½teaspoon paprika
- 1onion, chopped
- 2teaspoons grated fresh ginger
- 3teaspoons curry powder
- 1teaspoon Asian chili paste
- 2teaspoons ground coriander
- 1teaspoon sugar
- 4cups vegetable broth
- 1teaspoon salt
- ¼teaspoon cayenne pepper
- ¼teaspoon black pepper
- 3scallions, chopped
- ¼teaspoon ground turmeric
- 1tablespoon fresh lime juice
- Lime wedges, for serving

Directions:
1. Add the coconut milk, tofu, all the vegetables, lemon juice, spices, and herbs in an instant pot.
2. Mix well and Cooking Time: with the lid on for 8 minutes.
3. Serve hot.

PASTA

01. Saucy Brussels Macaroni
Preparation Time: 30 minutes
Servings: 2

Ingredients
- Macaroni: 1 cup (after cooking
- Brussels sprout: 1 cup halved
- Olive oil: 1 tbsp
- Almond milk: ½ cup
- Flour: 2 tbsp
- Green onion: 1 chopped
- Salt and pepper: as per your taste
- Dried oregano: 2 tbsp

Directions:
1. Cooking Time: pasta as per packet instructions
2. Preheat the oven to 400F
3. In a bowl, add Brussels sprouts and season with pepper and salt and brush with oil
4. Add them to the baking sheet and roast for 20 minutes
5. In a serving tray, spread pasta and top with roasted sprouts
6. In a small pan, heat almond milk and stir in

flour
7. Add pasta and sprouts to them and stir to thicken
8. Serve with oregano on top

Nutrition:
Carbs: 49.75g
Protein: 6.75g
Fats: 9.65g
Calories: 204Kcal

02. Simple Pasta With Chili Garlic Tarka

Preparation Time: 25 minutes
Servings: 2

Ingredients

- Pasta: 1 cup (after cooking
- Chickpeas: 1 cup can rinsed and drained
- Olive oil: 1 tbsp
- Garlic: 2 cloves minced
- Garlic: 3 cloves sliced
- Red onion: 1 small diced
- Parsley: ½ cup chopped
- Red chili flakes: 1 tsp
- Salt: 1 tsp
- Black pepper: ½ tsp
- Vegetable oil: 2 tbsp
- Cumin: 2 tbsp

Directions:

1. Cooking Time: pasta as per packet instructions
2. Take a saucepan and heat oil in it
3. Add minced garlic and onion to it and make them tender
4. Add salt and black pepper, stir
5. Add pasta and chickpeas and mix well

6. Lower the heat and cover and Cooking Time: for 5 minutes
7. In a separate small pan, pour vegetable oil and add sliced garlic and cumin
8. When garlic turn golden add red chili flakes and pour this mixture immediately on the top of the pasta

Nutrition:
Carbs: 41.2g
Protein: 11.25g
Fats: 23.6
Calories: 412Kcal

03. Spaghetti With Roasted Cauliflower

Preparation Time: 30 minutes

Servings: 2

Ingredients

- Spaghetti Pasta: 1 cup (after cooking
- Cauliflower florets: 1 cup
- Olive oil: 1 tbsp
- Salt and pepper: as per your taste

Directions:

1. Cooking Time: pasta as per packet instructions
2. Preheat the oven to 400F
3. In a bowl, add cauliflower and season with pepper and salt and brush with oil
4. Add them to the baking sheet and roast for 20 minutes
5. In a serving tray, spread pasta and top with roasted cauliflower
6. Serve with your favorite sauce

Nutrition:

Carbs: 21.2g

Protein: 4.8g

Fats: 17.9g

Calories: 172Kcal

04. Spicy Bean Pasta

Preparation Time: 30 minutes
Servings: 2

Ingredients

- Pasta: 1 cup (after cooking
- Spinach: 1 cup
- Beans: 1 cup can
- Green chili: 2 sliced
- Cayenne pepper: 1 tsp
- Garlic powder: ¼ tsp
- Tahini: 2 tbsp
- Onion: 1 small diced
- Salt: as per your taste
- Oil: 2 tbsp

Directions:

1. Cooking Time: pasta as per packet instructions
2. Take a pan and heat oil in it and add onion and green chili
3. Stir and Cooking Time: for 3-4 minutes
4. Now add spinach and beans and add salt, cayenne pepper, tahini, and garlic powder
5. Mix them all well and add pasta
6. Then reduce the heat and cover and Cooking Time: for 5 minutes

7. Remove from heat and serve hot

Nutrition:

Carbs: 51g

Protein: 15.4g

Fats: 25g

Calories: 389Kcal

05. Split Peas Pasta

Preparation Time: 50minutes

Servings: 2

Ingredients

- Pasta: 1 cup cooked
- Split peas: 1 cup
- Spinach: 1 cup
- Water: 6 cups
- Onion: 1 large coarsely chopped
- Garlic: 1 tbsp paste
- Fine sea salt: as per your taste

Directions:

1. Cooking Time: pasta as per packet instructions
2. Take a large saucepan and add water and bring to boil
3. Add the chopped onions, garlic paste, spinach, split peas, and salt and bring to boil
4. Lower the heat to medium and Cooking Time: for 30-35 minutes with partial cover
5. Add the mixture to the high-speed blender to make a puree
6. Whisk in water if desired
7. Add again to the pan and slowly heat on a low flame for 10-15 minutes
8. Add in pasta during the last minutes
9. Add herbs or spices in between to augment the taste

Nutrition:
Carbs: 64.9g
Protein: 21.95g
Fats: 1.95g
Calories: 352Kcal

SAUCES, AND CONDIMENTS

01. Thai Curry Sauce
Preparation Time: 7 Minutes
Servings: 6

Ingredients:
- 1 teaspoon coconut oil
- 2 ½ cup full-fat coconut milk
- 1 tablespoon mild curry sauce
- 1 cup vegetable stock
- 1 teaspoon coconut aminos
- 2 cloves garlic, minced
- 1 lemongrass stalk, bruised
- 1 tablespoon lime juice
- 4 tablespoons chopped cilantro

Directions:
1. Heat coconut oil in instant pot on Sauté.
2. Add garlic and curry paste and Cooking Time: 30 seconds.
3. Add remaining ingredients, and lock lid into place.
4. Select Manual and High-pressure 4 minutes.
5. Use a natural pressure release Directions.
6. Open the lid and strain into a bowl.

7. Serve or store into a fridge.

02. Sweet Peanut Sauce
Preparation Time: 35 Minutes
Servings: 4

Ingredients:
- 1 cup peanut butter, organic
- ½ cup peanut oil
- 1 teaspoon garlic powder
- 4 tablespoons maple syrup or coconut nectar
- 2 cups water
- 1 teaspoon chili flakes
- 1 tablespoon lime juice
- 1 teaspoon ground cumin
- ½ teaspoon ground fennel
- Salt, to taste

Directions:
1. Combine all ingredients into a food blender.
2. Blend until smooth.
3. Transfer the ingredients into Instant pot.
4. Lock lid into place and select Manual.
5. Low-pressure 30 minutes.
6. Use a natural pressure release Directions.
7. Open the lid and serve sauce.

03. Fast Hollandaise Sauce

Preparation Time: 5 Minutes
Servings: 4

Ingredients:

- ¼ cup fresh lemon juice
- 1 tablespoon nutritional yeast
- 1/3 cup Vegan mayonnaise
- 1 ½ tablespoons Dijon mustard
- 3 tablespoons almond milk
- 1 pinch salt
- 1 pinch black pepper
- 2 cups water

Directions:

1. Pour water into Instant pot and insert trivet.
2. Combine all ingredients into food blender.
3. Blend until smooth. Transfer into heat-proof bowl.
4. Place the bowl onto trivet and lock lid.
5. Select Sauté and adjust heat to More.
6. Steam 3 minutes.
7. Remove from the Instant pot and whisk with a wire whisk until fluffy.
8. Serve.

04. Red Pepper Sauce

Preparation Time: 25 Minutes
Servings: 4

Ingredients:

- 2 red bell peppers, sliced
- 1 tablespoon olive oil
- ¾ cup vegetable stock
- 4 tablespoons unsweetened almond milk
- Salt and pepper, to taste
- 2 shallots, sliced
- 2 cloves garlic, minced
- ½ teaspoon dried basil

Directions:

1. Heat oil in Instant pot on Sauté.
2. Add shallots and bell peppers.
3. Cooking Time: 4 minutes.
4. Add remaining ingredients and lock the lid.
5. Adjust heat to More, and Cooking Time: 20 minutes.
6. Open the lid and puree the bell peppers with immersion blender.
7. Serve or store into fridge.

05. Divine Green Sauce

Preparation Time: 25 Minutes
Servings: 4

Ingredients:

- 1 green chili pepper, seeded, chopped
- 12 tomatillos
- 2 shallots, diced
- 2 cloves garlic, peeled
- Salt and pepper, to taste
- 1 tablespoon cilantro, chopped
- ½ tablespoon parsley, chopped

Directions:

1. Place tomatillos into Instant pot.
2. Cover with water.
3. Lock the lid and Select Sauté. Adjust heat to More.
4. Cooking Time: tomatillos 20 minutes or until tender.
5. Open the lid and drain the tomatillos.
6. Place them into food processor, along with remaining ingredients.
7. Blend until smooth.
8. Pour back the mixture into the Instant pot. Cooking Time: on Sauté 5 minutes.
9. Serve or store in a fridge.

SNACKS

01. Avocado Tomato Bruschetta

Preparation Time: 10 minutes
Cooking Time: 0 minute
Servings: 4

Ingredients:

- 3 slices of whole-grain bread
- 6 chopped cherry tomatoes
- ½ of sliced avocado
- ½ teaspoon minced garlic
- ½ teaspoon ground black pepper
- 2 tablespoons chopped basil
- ½ teaspoon of sea salt
- 1 teaspoon balsamic vinegar

Directions:

1. Place tomatoes in a bowl, and then stir in vinegar until mixed. Top bread slices with avocado slices, then top evenly with tomato mixture, garlic and basil, and season with salt and black pepper.
2. Serve straight away

Nutrition:
Calories: 131 Cal
Fat: 7.3 g

Carbs: 15 g
Protein: 2.8 g
Fiber: 3.2 g

02. Butter Carrots

Preparation time: 10 minutes

Cooking time: 10 minutes

Total time: 20 minutes

Servings: 04

Ingredients:

- 2 cups baby carrots
- 1 tablespoon brown sugar
- ½ tablespoon vegan butter, melted
- A pinch each salt and black pepper

How to Prepare:

1. Take a baking dish suitable to fit in your air fryer.
2. Toss carrots with sugar, butter, salt and black pepper in the baking dish.
3. Place the dish in the air fryer basket and seal the fryer.
4. Cooking Time: the carrots for 10 minutes at 350 degrees F on air fryer mode.
5. Enjoy.

Nutritional Values:

Calories 119

Total Fat 14 g

Saturated Fat 2 g

Cholesterol 65 mg

Sodium 269 mg

Total Carbs 19 g

Fiber 4 g

Sugar 6 g

Protein 5g
03. Leeks With Butter

Preparation time: 10 minutes
Cooking time: 7 minutes
Total time: 17 minutes
Servings: 04

Ingredients:
- 1 tablespoon vegan butter, melted
- 1 tablespoon lemon juice
- 4 leeks, washed and halved
- Salt and black pepper to taste

How to Prepare:
1. Take a baking dish suitable to fit in your air fryer.
2. Toss the leeks with butter, salt, and black pepper in the dish.
3. Place the dish in the air fryer basket.
4. Seal the fryer and Cooking Time: the carrots for 7 minutes at 350 degrees F on air fryer mode.
5. Add a drizzle of lemon juice.
6. Mix well then serve.

Nutritional Values:
Calories 231
Total Fat 20.1 g
Saturated Fat 2.4 g
Cholesterol 110 mg
Sodium 941 mg
Total Carbs 20.1 g
Fiber 0.9 g
Sugar 1.4 g
Protein 4.6 g

04. Juicy Brussel Sprouts

Preparation time: 10 minutes
Cooking time: 10 minutes
Total time: 20 minutes
Servings: 04

Ingredients:
- 1-pound brussels sprouts, trimmed
- ¼ cup green onions, chopped
- 6 cherry tomatoes, halved
- 1 tablespoon olive oil
- Salt and black pepper to taste

How to Prepare:
1. Take a baking dish suitable to fit in your air fryer.
2. Toss brussels sprouts with salt and black pepper in the dish.
3. Place this dish in the air fryer and seal the fryer.
4. Cooking Time: the sprouts for 10 minutes at 350 degrees F on air fryer mode.
5. Toss these sprouts with green onions, tomatoes, olive oil, salt, and pepper in a salad bowl.
6. Devour.

Nutritional Values:
Calories 361
Total Fat 16.3 g
Saturated Fat 4.9 g
Cholesterol 114 mg
Sodium 515 mg
Total Carbs 29.3 g
Fiber 0.1 g
Sugar 18.2 g
Protein 3.3 g

05. Parsley Potatoes

Preparation time: 10 minutes
Cooking time: 10 minutes
Total time: 20 minutes
Servings: 4

Ingredients:
- 1-pound gold potatoes, sliced
- 2 tablespoons olive oil
- ¼ cup parsley leaves, chopped
- Juice from ½ lemon
- Salt and black pepper to taste

How to Prepare:
1. Take a baking dish suitable to fit in your air fryer.
2. Place the potatoes in it and season them liberally with salt, pepper, olive oil, and lemon juice.
3. Place the baking dish in the air fryer basket and seal it.
4. Cooking Time: the potatoes for 10 minutes at 350 degrees F on air fryer mode.
5. Serve warm with parsley garnishing.
6. Devour.

Nutritional Values:
Calories 205
Total Fat 22.7 g
Saturated Fat 6.1 g
Cholesterol 4 mg
Sodium 227 mg
Total Carbs 26.1 g
Fiber 1.4 g
Sugar 0.9 g
Protein 5.2 g

DESSERTS AND DRINKS

01. Oatmeal Cookies
Preparation Time: 20 Minutes
Servings: 18

Ingredients:
- 4 cups rolled oats, gluten-free
- ½ cup flaxseed oil
- 1 cup soy milk
- 1 tsp vanilla extract
- ½ cup agave nectar
- 1 cup rice flour
- 1 tsp xanthan gum
- ½ tsp baking soda
- ¼ cup stevia

Directions:
1. In a large mixing bowl, combine soy milk. Flaxseed oil, vanilla extract and agave nectar. Stir until combined and set aside.
2. In a separate bowl, combine the remaining ingredients and stir well.
3. Now, combine wet and dry ingredients and stir again until you get a nice batter.
4. Fill the stainless steel insert of your instant pot with ½ inch of water. Position a trivet and place the springform pan on top. Drop the

tablespoon-sized portions of the batter onto the pan.

5. Close the lid and plug in your instant pot. Cover with a lid and set the steam release handle. Press "Manual" button and set the timer for 5 minutes. Cooking Time: on high pressure.

6. When done, press "Cancel" button and release the steam naturally. Let it cool before serving.

7. Enjoy!

02. Cherry Spread
Preparation Time: 20 Minutes
Servings: 10

Ingredients:
- 1 cup fresh cherries, pitted and chopped
- 1 lb silken tofu
- ½ cup powdered sugar
- 3 tbsp all-purpose flour
- 1 tsp xanthan gum

Directions:
1. Combine tofu, sugar, flour, and xanthan gum in a food processor. Blend until combined and transfer to the stainless steel insert of your instant pot.
2. Plug in your instant pot and press "Sautee" button and stir in the flour. Cooking Time: for 5 minutes and then add 1 cup water.
3. Close the lid and press "Manual" button. Set the steam release handle and set the timer for 5 minutes. Cooking Time: on high pressure.
4. When done, press "Cancel" button and turn off the pot. Perform a quick release and open the pot. Let it chill for a while before serving.
5. Store the cherry spread in the air-tight containers and refrigerate up to 2 weeks.
6. Enjoy!

03. Creamy Coconut Eggs

Preparation Time: 20 Minutes
Servings: 10

Ingredients:

- 4 oz vegan cheese cream cheese
- 1 cup powdered sugar
- ¾ cup mashed potatoes
- 6 oz silken tofu
- 1 tsp coconut extract
- 2 cups vegan chocolate chips
- 1 ½ cup shredded coconut, unsweetened

Directions:

1. Combine tofu and vegan cream cheese in a food processor and pulse until smooth and creamy. Add sugar, mashed potatoes, and coconut extract. Pulse again for one minute to combine. Transfer all to a large mixing bowl and stir in the shredded coconut. Mix with your hands until fully combined. Refrigerate the mixture for 15 minutes.
2. Line a springform pan with some cooking paper. Spoon the mixture into egg-shaped pieces. Freeze for about 10-15 minutes.
3. Melt the chocolate chips and drizzle over the egg-shaped pieces.
4. Fill the ½ inch water in the stainless steel insert

of your instant pot. Place the trivet on the bottom and place the springform on top. Close the lid and plug in your instant pot. Set the steam release handle and press "Manual" button and set the timer for 5 minutes.

5. When done, press "Cancel" and turn off the pot. Release the pressure naturally.
6. Chill well before serving.

04. Pumpkin Pancakes

Preparation Time: 20 Minutes
Servings: 6

Ingredients:
- 1 cup buckwheat flour
- 2 tsp baking powder
- 2 cups pumpkin, chopped
- ½ cup rice milk
- 1 tbsp egg replacer
- ½ tsp salt
- 1 tsp cinnamon, ground
- 1 tsp stevia
- ½ cup agave nectar

Directions:
1. In a medium-sized mixing bowl, combine rice milk and egg replacer. Beat well with a whisking attachment on high speed. Gradually, add buckwheat flour, pumpkin puree, baking powder, salt, cinnamon, and stevia powder. Continue to beat until combined.
2. Plug in your instant pot and grease the stainless steel insert with some oil. Spoon 2-3 tablespoons of batter into the pot. Close the lid and set to low pressure. Press "Manual" button and set the timer for 5 minutes.

3. When done, press "Cancel" and perform a quick release. Repeat the process with the remaining batter.
4. Top each pancake with some agave nectar and enjoy immediately.

05. Orange Dessert

Preparation Time: 45 Minutes
Servings: 10

Ingredients:

- ½ cup all-purpose flour
- 2 cups brown sugar
- 2 cups olive oil
- 1 tbsp egg replacer
- 1 tsp baking powder

Orange topping:

- 3 cups powdered sugar
- 5 cups water
- 1 cup freshly squeezed orange juice
- 1 tbsp orange zest
- 1 large orange, sliced

Directions:

1. In a large bowl, combine egg replacer with brown sugar, oil, and baking powder. Gradually add flour until the mixture is thick and slightly sticky. Using your hands, shape the balls and flatten them to half-inch thick.
2. Place in a fitting springform pan and plug in your instant pot. Pour two cups of water in a stainless steel insert and position a trivet on the bottom. Gently place the springform pan onto

the trivet. Cover the springform pan with foil and seal the lid. Set the steam release handle and press the "Manual" button. Set the timer for 20 minutes.

3. When done, press "Cancel" button and perform a quick release. Open and gently remove the springform and foil. Cool to a room temperature.

4. Now, add the remaining sugar, water, orange juice, orange zest, and orange slices in your instant pot. Press the "Sautee" button and gently simmer until the sugar dissolves. Press "Cancel" button and remove the orange mixture.

5. Pour the hot topping over chilled dessert and set aside, allowing it to soak the orange dressing.

06. Chocolate Bundt Cake

Preparation Time: 45Minutes
Servings: 8

Ingredients:

- 2 cups all-purpose flour
- ¾ cup cocoa powder
- 2 cups natural cane sugar
- 1 tsp baking soda
- ½ tsp salt
- 1 cup coconut oil, melted
- ½ cup coconut cream
- ¾ cup coconut milk
- 1 cup silken tofu

Directions:

1. In a large bowl, combine together all dry ingredients.
2. Place coconut oil, coconut cream, coconut milk, and tofu in a large mixing bowl. With a paddle attachment on, beat well on high speed until light and fluffy.
2. Slowly add the flour mixture and continue to beat until fully combined.
3. Spray a 6 cup bundt pan with some cooking spray and pour the mixture in it. Wrap the pan tightly with aluminum foil and set aside.
4. Add 2 cups of water in the stainless steel insert

of your pot and place the trivet inside.

5. Place the wrapped bundt pan on top and seal the lid.

6. Press the 'Manual' button and set the timer to 35 minutes.

7. When you hear the cooker's end signal, release the pressure naturally and open the lid.

8. Cool to a room temperature before removing the cake from the pan.

07. Chocolate Berry Cake

Preparation Time: 35Minutes
Servings: 6

Ingredients:

- 2 cups oat flour
- 2 tbsp shredded coconut
- 1 ½ tsp baking soda
- 1/3 cup cocoa powder
- ¼ tsp salt
- 3 cups silken tofu
- 1 tsp vanilla extract
- 1 cup coconut milk
- 3 cups soy yogurt
- 1 cup almond cream
- 5 oz vegan dark chocolate, melted
- 2 tsp agave nectar
- 1 tsp vanilla extract

Directions:

1. Brush a 7-inch pan with some oil and line with parchment paper. Set aside.
2. In a large mixing bowl, combine together oat flour, shredded coconut, baking soda, cocoa powder, and salt. Mix well and add tofu, vanilla extract, and soy milk. With a dough hook attachment, beat well for 3 minutes.
3. Transfer the batter into the prepared baking

pan and set aside.

4. Add one cup of water to your instant pot and place the trivet. Gently place the pan onto the trivet and close the lid.

5. Set the steam release handle and press the 'Manual' button. Set the timer to 25 minutes.

6. When you hear the cooker's end signal, perform a quick release and open the lid. Remove the pan from the cooker and cool to a room temperature.

7. Meanwhile, in a bowl of a stand mixer, combine soy yogurt, almond cream, melted chocolate, agave nectar, and vanilla extract. Using a whisking attachment, beat well on high speed for 3 minutes.

8. Pour the mixture over chilled crust and refrigerate for 1 hour before serving.

08. Mocha Brownies

Preparation Time: 30Minutes
Servings: 8

Ingredients:

- 2 cups oat flour
- ¼ cup shredded coconut
- 1 ½ tsp baking soda
- 1/3 cup cocoa powder
- ¼ tsp salt
- 1 tsp vanilla extract
- 1 tsp stevia powder
- ¾ cup coconut milk
- ¼ cup instant coffee
- 3 tbsp ground flaxseed
- ¼ cup water
- 1 cup soy yogurt
- 1 cup almond yogurt, vanilla flavored
- 1/3 cup shredded coconut
- 1 tsp vanilla extract

Directions:

1. Spray a 7-inch springform pan with some cooking spray and line with parchment paper. Set aside
2. In a large mixing bowl, mix together flour, shredded coconut, baking soda, cocoa powder,

salt, and stevia powder. Add vanilla extract, coconut milk, and coffee. Using a paddle attachment beat well on high speed until fully incorporated.

3. Meanwhile, whisk together flaxseed and water. Pour the mixture into the bowl and continue to mix for 2 minutes.

4. Pour the mixture into the prepared springform pan and set aside.

5. Pour two cups of water into your instant pot and set the trivet. Place the springform pan onto trivet and seal the cooker's lid.

6. Press the 'Manual' button and set the timer to 20 minutes. When done, release the pressure naturally and open the lid.

7. Gently remove the springform pan from your instant pot and place on a wire rack to cool.

8. Meanwhile, combine the remaining ingredients in a mixing bowl and whisk together until fully combined. Optionally add 1 teaspoon of instant coffee for some more flavor.

9. Pour the mixture over chilled crust and refrigerate for one hour before serving.

09. Caramel Shortbread

Preparation Time: 50 Minutes
Servings: 6
Ingredients:

For the crust
- 1 ½ cup all-purpose flour
- 2 tsp stevia powder
- 1 cup coconut oil

For the caramel layer:
- 1 cup natural cane sugar
- ½ cup almond butter
- 2 tbsp agave nectar
- 1 cup almond milk, unsweetened

For the chocolate topping:
- 1 cup vegan chocolate, melted
- ½ cup coconut cream

Directions:

1. In a large bowl, combine flour, stevia, and coconut oil. Beat well with an electric mixer on low. Using your hands, combine the dough evenly until crumbly. Press into 7-inch pan and wrap tightly with aluminum foil.

2. Pour 1 cup of water in your instant pot and set the trivet. Place wrapped pan onto trivet and seal the lid. Set the timer for 20 minutes.

3. When you hear the cooker's end signal, release the pressure naturally and open the lid. Gently remove the springform pan and remove the foil.
4. Meanwhile, combine sugar, butter, agave, and milk in a large bowl. Gently bring it to a boil over medium heat and simmer for 7-10 minutes, or until it begins to firm. Pour the warm mixture over crust and cool completely.
5. Finally, prepare the chocolate layer. Melt the chocolate in a double broiler or in a microwave. Stir in coconut cream and pour the mixture over chilled shortbread.

10. Easy Hazelnut Cake

Preparation Time: 90 Minutes
Servings: 8
Ingredients:

For the crust:

- ½ almond flour
- ¼ cup cocoa powder, unsweetened
- 1 tsp baking powder
- 1 tsp stevia powder
- ½ cup almond milk
- ½ cup almond butter
- 4 tbsp chia seeds

For the topping:

- 2 cups almond yogurt
- ¼ cup cocoa powder
- ½ cup vegan dark chocolate, melted
- ¼ cup grated hazelnuts

Directions:

1. Line 3 8-inches round pans with parchment paper. Dust with some flour and set aside.
2. In a medium-sized bowl, combine almond flour, cocoa powder, baking powder, and stevia. Whisk together and gradually add milk. With a paddle attachment on, beat well for 2-3 minutes. Finally, add almond butter and continue to beat

95

for 3 minutes. Pour the batter into prepared pans.

3. Add 2 cups of water in your pressure cooker and set the trivet. Place one pan in your pressure cooker and seal the lid. Set the 'Manual' mode for 20 minutes.

4. When you hear the cooker's end signal, perform a quick release and open the lid. Repeat the process with the remaining 2 pans. Cool each crust to a room temperature.

5. Meanwhile, combine almond yogurt, cocoa powder, melted chocolate, and hazelnuts. Spread the mixture over each crust, creating layers.

6. Refrigerate for one hour before serving.

CONCLUSION

Thanks for making to the end! I hope you enjoy all the recipes herein. If dieting seems very important to you and you need to do it right, then it is recommended that you visit a professional such as a nutritionist or dietitian to discuss your dieting plan and optimizing it for the better.

No matter how much you want to lose weight, it is not advised that you decrease your calorie intake to an unhealthy level. Losing weight does not mean that you stop eating. It is done by carefully planning meals.

A plant-based diet is very easy once you get into it. At first, you will start to face a lot of difficulties, but if you start slowly, then you can face all the barriers and achieve your goal.

CPSIA information can be obtained
at www.ICGtesting.com
Printed in the USA
BVHW040753060221
599462BV00006B/124